Chocolate Covered Cherries

By

Shelbie M. Moore

Cover Art: Justin Pollard

Cover Design: Brittany J. Jackson

Illustrations: Chasity Douglas and Justin Pollard

Published by G Publishing, LLC
P. O. Box 24374
Detroit, MI 48224

ISBN 13: 978-0-9843426-1-7
ISBN 10: 0-9843426-1-3

Library of Congress Control Number: 2009912603

Printed in the United States of America

Sweet Learning (Introduction)

This book of poetry
Is the second one I've wrote
"Live the life you want"
Is my favorite quote

This quote's meaning is simple
Do anything you want to do
Things like money, age, or race
Should never distract you

The reason I titled this book
After a treat so delicious
Is because most of my poems remind me
Of things so addicting and nutritious

The *Cookie Crumbs* section is sad
But if you need some old fashioned lovin'
Skip past the *Homemade Dishes*
To a section called *Sweet Nothings*

The *Full Courses* tell short stories
Read the *Sock-It-To-Me Cakes* for a laugh
The *Family Recipes* share a smile
All the things people need to have

This book is filled with empathy
Be careful reading the text
Because once you read one poem
You'll want to read the rest

I dedicate this book to Justin, Chasity, Bryan, and DeVonte'.
Thanks for all your help by making this book everything I
wanted it to be and more.
I love you guys.
<3 Shelbie
aka Jelli and Angel

p.s . . .

*"All errors, inconsistencies, and out-and-out screw-ups are purely the
fault of my agent, editor, publisher, and anyone else who messed with my
book before it made it into your hands."*
-Allison van Diepen

(She had a point . . .)

Shelbie M. Moore

Family Recipes

…poems about the love of family and friends

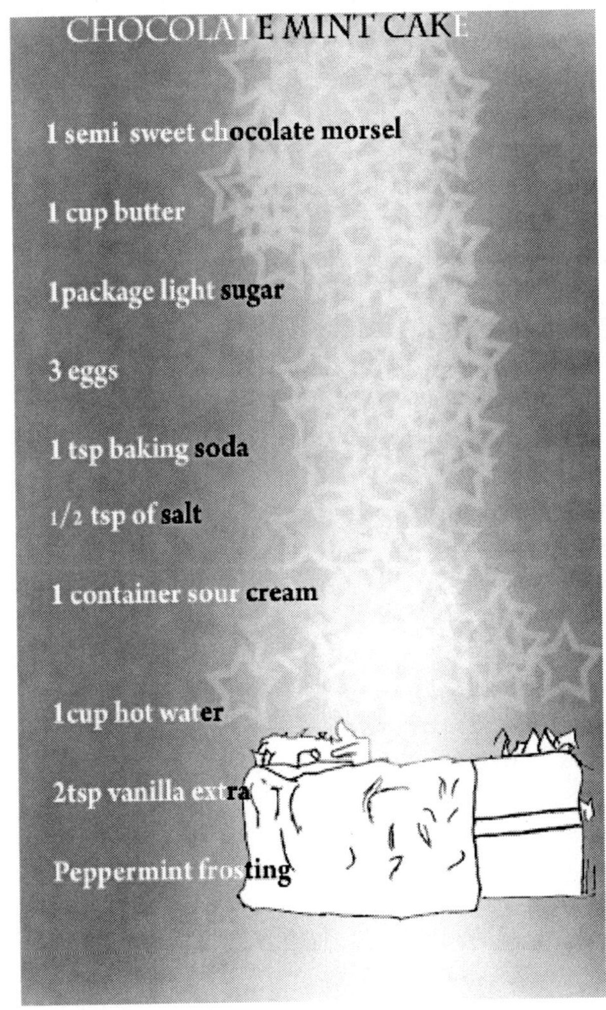

Send Me A Butterfly Kiss

Send me a butterfly kiss
With your thick lashes and blue wings
Send me a butterfly kiss
With your soft eyes and sweet things

Send me a butterfly kiss
With your cute smile and innocence
Send me a butterfly kiss
With your small nose and childish rinse

Send me a butterfly kiss
Let your warmness hit my cheeks
Send me a butterfly kiss
Let your kindness and love leak

Send me a butterfly kiss
Let your words be with your eye lashes
Send me a butterfly kiss
Let your sweetness give me flashes

Send me a butterfly kiss
For every time I see you
Send me a butterfly kiss
For every time I need you

Send me a butterfly kiss
Because your love is so pure
Send me a butterfly kiss
Because it eases my torture

Send me a butterfly kiss
Right away, my dearest daughter
I need your butterfly kiss
To make me bigger and stronger

Shelbie M. Moore

Humming Honey Bee

Old bees and new bees
Flowing gently through the breeze

All those bees feel the need
To take a taste of my honey

My fresh honey comb
Is still very new
All those busy bees
Want to stir my honey stew

Sweet to the taste
My honey is rare
I tease those buzzing bees
They can only stare

My wings flap loosely
Training those bees' eyes
To let them know my honey comb
Is the perfect shape and size

The queen bee once told me
Baby bee, protect your honey

Especially from those buzzing bees
Who'll only want to taste and leave

Shelbie M. Moore

In Mama's Kitchen

In my mama's kitchen
They are so many things
Recipes and side notes
All hanging by a string

Pictures of the family
Windows showing light
Dishes fill the sink
From the previous night

But cooking and cleaning
Weren't all that lied within
There were so many other things
In my mother's special den

There were many stories
From way back when
From when I was one
Until when I was ten

There were dried up stains
From blood on the floor
There were concealed cracks
From the slamming of the doors

There were artistic posters
Of her calming bands
There were bad memories
Of her latest man

When you walk in
You see a place of meals
When I walk in
I see my mama's past revealed

Chocolate Covered Cherries

Take My Traits

Baby, look past my face
And take a look at my traits

Born from different dark and tan bodies
Too black for the suburbs
Too white for the hood
Too ghetto for the whites
Too proper for the blacks
Teased by the things that people say
But I made it
So, my baby
Take my strength

Born around competition
All men and women
Have envy
About you and me
I know when to yell
And how to be cool
I try to stay calm
As others act a fool
So, my baby
Take my attitude

Born with strawberry lips
Smacking in tangy taste
Styling with radiant color
Attracting the right attention
Two straight rows of pearly teeth
Both sides surrounded by chubby cheeks
So, my baby
Take my smile

                              Shelbie M. Moore

Born with a family
And friends who show concern
My selfless ways
Caring and helping others
Putting you first
As my mother did for me
Out of all the traits you choose of
Just remember, my baby
Take my love

From Your Parent Or Guardian

A lot more than love
Goes into a relationship
There is yelling and screaming
Often coming from your lips

There is the pressure
Of touching or sex
There are hurtful things transferred
From one party to the next

I'd like you to wait
Until you're absolutely sure
I don't want you
To become un-pure

Let me assure you
I've been there, sweetie
I'm not saying you're irresponsible
I'm saying I'm not ready

Shelbie M. Moore

Rest In Peace
(For Kaleigh Marie Moore)

I never knew you
But I feel I've seen you before
You are very famous
Ms. Kaleigh Marie Moore

Friends still talk of you
Haters still hate
I even hear you exes say
They miss the girl they used to date

You were beautiful
I've seen from your pictures
I'm not stalking your soul
Just complimenting a sistah

Brown skin, big eyes
You sound a little like me
Hey, our last names are to same
So we have a few similarities

Like I said before
I never met you
But I feel a connection
That has to be true

Whether family or friend
Foe or lover
Cousin or Aunt
Sister or mother

A tree still grows at Summit
To remind us all
That the great Ms. Moore
Once stood tall

Born 11.28.92
Left 09.12.07
But it'll be okay baby
Because I'll meet you in heaven

                        Shelbie M. Moore

Childhood Toy

There's one person
You keep close to you
Like that childhood toy
From when you were two

You squeeze it, hug it
And talk to it daily
You make presents for it
And you treat it like a baby

I have that one friend
Who'll never leave me
Who will stand by my side
And who will always believe me

If I'm on the stand
He'll take my defense
If I'm washing a car
He's there to rinse

He's really compassionate
He's always there
He's a great friend
He's my teddy bear

Homies For Life

Someone once asked me
When I called them my homie
"Is that all I am to you?"
And I had to break it down
And let him know that this was true

Because in my book
A homie is for life
Buddies come and go
Friends don't always show
But a homie in my book
Is someone who'll never say no

A homie to me
Will never be an enemy
A homie is like family
A homie is the cure
To all my hurt and torture
They advise me when I'm unsure
And they love me

And I replied to this person
With "You could be a friend
Someone who's not always there to the end
Someone who will close the door and leave
But as a homie you hold the key
A homie will be sweet and never tart
A homie is a word that has heart"

Shelbie M. Moore

Magnificent Macaroni

My Grandmama's Macaroni
Is as delicious as can be
She adds 4 cups of milk
And a tea spoon of honey

Paprika on the top
Baked cheese on the sides
Brown sugar sprinkled lightly
Noodles mixed inside

The way she stirs
The way she cooks
The way it smells
The way it looks

I like all her creations
Like her Southern Mostacolli
But I could fall in love
With my Grandmama's Macaroni

My Priceless Friends

I have a friend named Garnet
Who is very successful
He makes 100,000 a year
On selling designer utensils

He's never been in an accident
He'll make you smile for weeks
His popularity is amazing
And has a perfect physic

Amethyst is my best friend
She's a healer of the sick
She'll cure every sore
From PMS to Syphilis

A nice and sweet soul
And likes to play it safe
Never drinks, never smokes
She knows how to behave

Aquamarine is beautiful
With piercing blue eyes
Her meditation powers
Will blow your mind!

She's from Brazil
Her silence can be curious
Her answers to life's questions
Could make your mind delirious

I am Emerald!
The lucky one of my friends
We're all priceless together
For extraordinary reason

                    Shelbie M. Moore

Sock-It-To-Me Cakes

*...poems about silly and sarcastic things
or about common sense*

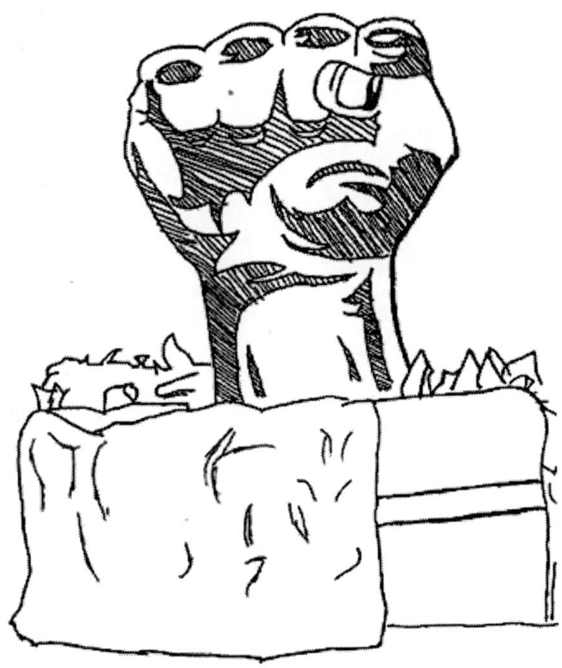

95%

Boy, from a far
Your eyes look magical
I am taken, I know
And I'm 95% faithful

The remaining 5%
Is the fault of my eyes
They wander around daily
And check out other guys

When we are not together
My eyes see other features
Likes the muscles God bestowed
On his beautiful creatures

Big arms, ripped legs
Full lips, strong thighs
Big feet, ripped abs
Small waist, green eyes

I say, "Boyfriend, don't worry.
My heart belongs to you."
But my eyes will always wander
To someone brand new

Shelbie M. Moore

Blowing Bubbles and Kicking Rocks

You know what?
Since you want to make fun of me
You can suck a lemon
And go kiss a monkey!

Go fly a red kite
In a Katrina-like-hurricane
Go climb a Christmas tree
And choke on candy cane!

Go blow a bubble
With Spongebob and Patrick
Go kick rocks
With Batman's side kick!

Take yourself to the Devil's home
In gasoline covered pants
Travel to the furthest park
And go sit on red ants!

Yes, I know very well
I sound like a child
But you will get in trouble
For talking so foul

You see, we're in the middle school
And in case you didn't get the hint
Their principal heard you call me
A word that rhymes with "witch"

And with that vulgar mouth
You'll have to talk your way
Out of suspension and detention
And I'll get away

Chocolate Covered Cherries

Enjoy "In-School Suspension"
Enjoy missing that class
I'm going home, and you . . .
Can fall on a bed of glass!

                    Shelbie M. Moore

Backstabbers

"You're so jealous!"
My twin sister screamed
"Because he thinks I'm nice
And he thinks your mean!"

"He said my eyes were magical
He's not like other guys."
I tried my very hardest
Not to roll my eyes

"He adores my clothes
And my flowing locks."
I chuckled under my breath
She stomped and yelled, "Stop!"

"We hug all the time
And we blow each other kisses."
I listened as I thought,
She'll never be his Mrs.

I tried not to break my frown
But when she said, "He loves me."
I threw back my head with laughter and said
"That's what he told me!"

The Joker
(For *The Dark Knight* fans)

I understand the sorrow
Brought on by my weapon
I understand the fear
That you might have drunken poison

I understand the regret
Of giving up her name
I understand the hurt
Of the blade in your brain

I understand the insanity
Of my crazy ways
I understand the genius
Of my intelligent phase

I understand your depression
Brought on by my madness
But, still, I'll ask you
Why so serious?

Shelbie M. Moore

Intewayz
(For Mr. Pierson, one of my favorite teachers)

What I live by is . . .

With every kiss blown
Peace sign thrown
And heart shaped
The world becomes
A better place

However . . .

Around the 1930's and 40's
There was this thing going on
The Great Depression?
Maybe you've heard of it

The only reason the Great Depression came to an
End
Was because this little thing called
WW2 (World War Two)
Created jobs
For pretty much everyone

Then the soldiers came back
After a few years
They missed their wives
One thing led to another

Intewayz . . .

The baby boom happened
Around the 1950's
More people got jobs!
Crib makers
People making baby blankets
Formula manufactures

Those babies are a little older now
And those darn baby boomers
They live to be so darn
Old
Because research technicians
Do their jobs
And find cures for
Diseases and such

Intewayz . . .

They need social security
That means people need more jobs
Before we go into another
Great Depression

Intewayz . . .

My question is
Do we have another war
To make peace
Or do we stay peaceful
And wait for a war
Against ourselves
To get out of this mess
Again . . .

                    Shelbie M. Moore

Speaking Teenager

Huh? Who?
She said what?!
Her hair is a mess!
Becky! Look at her butt!

L8R G8R
TTYL
BRB, OMG
LOL

I hate my teacher!
Can I have some water?
I can't work with her
He is a stalker!

Check out her new purse!
Look at his jeans!
What are you looking at?
Why are you so mean?

He's really cute
He's real fine
Time to make my move
Back off! He's mine!

For my language class essay
Which you said was due today
I wrote of the language of teenagers
So, like, can I have an A?

**Imagination
(For The Library)**

I saddled up my horse
One…two…three…go!
Zoom! Zoom!
It rode down the trails

Me and Rose
Deliver packages to their addresses
We stop by "the box"
To pick up more

Skert! We just missed a pedestrian!
The babies and adults
Always have the most deliveries
The teachers want their references
The parents want their recipes

Passing by familiar faces
Waving but keeping my pace
Rose is strong
But she can't handle the next load
So I grab Black Beauty
To take control

Checking in my new arrivals
Making sure they're still in style
Checking to see if they even belong to me…
"Shelbie?" said my co-worker.

I blinked and looked up from my desk
"You have to straighten the books around 386"

I stood up and grabbed my cart
My favorite one
With the rose sticker
Double checking to make sure
I wasn't on the drop chart

What? Don't give me those humiliating looks
What would you do to pass the time
If your minimum wage job
Was to put up books?

                                    Shelbie M. Moore

Diary Entry of a Gold Digger

He loves me
I love him not
I think he's ugly
He thinks I'm hot

He loves my scent
I think he's putrid
He thinks I'm nice
I think he's stupid

He shows me off
So they can all see
I want to leave him…
Wait! Is that Lexus for me?

Guess What I Love

I love how you cry
More than me at the movies
I like how you look down
To analyze my boobies

I adore how you continue
To leave the seat up
I idealize when you
Ask me to spell "I Cup"

I worship your soul
When you make me pay for dinner
And I just love you to say
I haven't gotten any thinner

So, what do you love about me?
Do you adore my nails, my limbs,
My mind, my smile,
Oh! How about my sarcasm?

Shelbie M. Moore

Spitting Game

He Said:
Shawty wat it do?
I kno you saw me checkin on you
I gotta say bae
Yo body is banging
Bump the dime you a dolla
Aye girl, let me holla
Iight I can respect that
Dis aint game I'm spitting
I don't just wanna tap dat
You could be ma wifey
Ma swagg wit yo style
We could be all dat baby
I got a crib bae
I get paid bae
I don't roll wit dem hataz bae
I'ma real nigga
I dont be pullin dat trigger
Dat aint fo me bae
You fo me
Wat it do shawty?
Wat cha say to that?

She Said:
I don't know what to say
Because I have no idea what you just said

Cookie Crumbs

...poems about the ups and downs we all feel

Shelbie M. Moore

Why Can't I Cry (Part 2)

I asked myself
Why couldn't I cry
I asked the reason
I kept asking why

Then I realized
Why my tears wouldn't flow
It was just because
It wasn't time to show

I loved you once
I love you still
Now when I hear your name
I'm a weeping willow

Memories are remembered
And thoughts are had
Not being with you
Makes me quite sad

I now know the reason
Why I couldn't cry
I wasn't ready to leave
And now I know why

Envious

Should the color of green
Be written on my face...
As I think of the thoughts
Trying to be erased...

No it shouldn't however
God holds the paint...
He knows my thoughts
So dry and taint...

He takes his brush
Against my skin...
And here we go
Back to green again...

Shelbie M. Moore

Playing With My Heart

You said we were done
Then laughed and said just playing
Then you said it again
A day later we were dating

You told me so many things
Including calling me out my name
Somehow I forgave you
And we continued our little game

One day, you said it softy
Like you were scared
Of how I would react
Will she be calm or aware?

Then you didn't say just joking
And you didn't apologize
You never repeated your jokes
And you said, "This wasn't a lie"

We've both chuckled
We've both lied
We got over it all
We really did try

Again, you asked me
To be your number one
Did I want to stay?
Or did I want to run?

I thought about the things
That you were so used to saying
Then I realized I'm too old
To just keep on playing

Chocolate Covered Cherries

From The Backseat

Being in a relationship
Is overrated
Long talks
Short walks
It's good for a while
Then it's finished

Being dumped
Being the dumper
Emotionally there is no difference
Heart crashing
Mood changing
Diet increasing
Happiness deceasing
Then you move on

Being single
The advantage
To flirt
Wink at the boys
Smile at the girls
Sway your hips
Getting numbers
And bigger tips

Being in the backseat
Watching your friend
Kiss her boyfriend goodnight
Makes you wish
For one moment
You had someone
To hold you that tight

                              Shelbie M. Moore

"Her"

She is gone forever
She left me
She was a bad girl
Why couldn't I see?

She was never truthful
She stood behind closed doors
She always stole
She threw my heart to the floor

I can't really hate her
It's more like dislike
I was even preparing
To make her my wife

I can't believe she did this
I want to stop thinking of her
There's just one problem
I'm still in love with her

In My Sweater

"No! No! No!
I just want to be friends
This isn't right
Let go of my hand!"

"We've gotten along fine
Let's not complicate things
I'm honestly too young
To be wearing a ring"

"Yes I do like you
I care about you too
But love is on a level
I can't climb too"

He jumped off his knee
And brought their lips together
She felt his small tears
Drip onto her sweater

When she left he thought
"I'm going to miss her"
When she left she thought
"Damn, he was a good kisser"

She wanted to stay
She had to leave
What would you have done
If his tears were on your sleeve?

                    Shelbie M. Moore

Wash It Away

Splash, splash, splash
The sound of the shower's rain
Fell against my grime
As I tried to wash away
My unforgivable crime

Scrub, scrub, scrub
I can't erase the memory of the night
I try so hard to come clean
Not just for myself
Because my dark light must be seen

Rinse, rinse, rinse
Please let the drugs run, *stampede*
Out of my arm
My legs still ache
My memories still gives my son harm

Rub, rub, rub
"I'm so sorry baby"
My tears still pour down my body
I know you are gone
Now I am a lady with nobody

I slept in the same towel
I used to try my rain
Knowing the night was bad
Knowing he'll never be a dad
Knowing I can't wash it away
I curl up and cry pain
Wishing God will forgive me
For losing the life of my unborn baby

Shelbie M. Moore

The Girl and The Guy

"It's lovely here," she said.
"It's my favorite place," he replied.
"Do you really have to leave?" she begged.
"I have to go to the office," he lied.

They shared a kiss goodbye
She went back to her spot
That garden was so beautiful
She wanted to rewind the clock

He walked into his room
Feeling awful about his fib
His new, gorgeous maid
Had left him lunch in bed

He had to get ready
Before he was late to dinner
Her friend had called with gossip
It made her body quiver

He knocked on the door, confidence
She opened it wider, anger
"Who was that woman?" she screamed.
"Walking around your manor?"

Something was wrong
He was so confused
He tried to explained
But she refused

After the door slammed
He was very depressed
Since he lied to get the time
To get the ring to match her dress

Chocolate Covered Cherries

It's Time to Go

Everyday you used to call
Now it's every week
Every morning we'd talk for hours
Now you never speak

Every night you'd say
You'd hate us to end
Now every month you say
We should be just friends

Everyday of every year
It's something new
Whatever happened to
Saying I love you?

You don't have to say it again
Because I know you love me
But the real question states
Do you still need me?

Do you need my kisses?
Do you need my hugs?
Do you need my laughter?
Do you need my love?

I think this answer
Is now and forever no
I hate to know that as I hold you
You want me to let go

So, since you won't
I'll do it for you
"I think it's time
That we stay friends too."

Shelbie M. Moore

Ain't It a Shame?

Ain't it a shame
When daddies become more like distant uncles?
Ain't it a shame
When a child gets hit by grown knuckles?

Ain't it a shame
When young kids have to act grown?
Ain't it a shame
When kids don't feel safe at home?

Ain't it a shame
When babies have more pain than sinners?
Ain't it a shame
That babies have to pray for dinner?

Ain't it a shame
When children are worked like slaves on a field?
And it's a damn shame
That a child knows how this feels

Dear Body

Stop it!
Stop making me this way!
Stop telling me to whine
When I'm doing okay

Stop making your language
Seem so confusing
Stop making me question
The things I'm choosing

I'm fine! I'm fine!
Goddamnit I'm cool!
Stop making my friends question
My actions at school!

I don't want to remember
About what happened days ago
It's all in the past
I've let it go!

You show how I'm feeling
And my spirit continues to drop
I'm begging you body
Please, just stop

                    Shelbie M. Moore

Remember

I don't remember
I can't remember
I want to remember
I need to remember

Yesterday was a flash
A light that blinded my thoughts
I can't remember what I said
I can't remember what I sought

But one little thing
Is in the back of my brain
But that one little thing
Is keeping me sane

It was a pair of lips
And eyes so clear
Those eyes starred at me
With admiration and fear

Those lips whispered,
"Try to remember"
Then I was told
I went into a deep slumber

Then…wait?
Where am I?
Why do I remember
Full lips and bright eyes?

Shouldn't Have To Learn This

Cheating…
It's like a knife
Of distrust
Of disloyalty
Of dishonor

And that knife
Gets jabbed into your heart so fast
That you can't think
You can't breathe
All you can do is see red
See the fires of hell
Burning…towering…
To the top of your eyes
It is madness

Were you got not good enough?
Were they better?
What went wrong?

Never been cheated on?
Good
Because
I found out
It sucks

                    Shelbie M. Moore

Good and Bad Days

Fighting
Non-stop bickering
Mistakes
Non-stop snickering

Carelessness
Non-stop shrugging
Making up
Non-stop hugging

Good days
Bad days
Either or will come
With a brand new day

But those bad days
Can out-weigh the good
I wouldn't delete them
Even if I could

Because without those days
Those days of bad
He would never know
What made me sad

When he mocks me
That non-stop judgment
It makes me want to loose faith
In our constant loving

I won't give up
Even with the rolling eyes
The stabs in the back
The many goodbyes

Because I love him
I know he loves me
The good days come often
But the bad ones come constantly

At the end of the day
I want to toss the ring
But when he calls me
My heart begins to sing

That's when I remember
All of the days
Our wonderful times
Our childish ways

I smile, laugh it off
Wipe the sobs away
Go to sleep, wake up
And live another day

Shelbie M. Moore

Understand My Eyes

Baby, try to understand why
Baby, look into my eyes

It's just, he looked at me
The way you used to
He sounded sincere
When he said, "I love you"

He smiled at me
He held me so close
Baby, understand why
I could not say no

I'm so thrown off
Or, at least I was
But remember baby
Every effect has a cause

You ignored me!
You wouldn't talk to me!
I'm not blaming you
For my adultery

It's just, that silence
No noise at all
It made me so depressed
It made me want to bawl

You used to like me
You couldn't have enough of me
Try to understand
Why I did it baby

I needed attention
That you wouldn't give
I needed fun
I needed to live!

I will not argue
If you want to leave
At least I'll know
You heard my plea

I didn't know what I had
I want your touch
I need your love
I miss you so much

Please, just talk to me
Look at me again
Hug me daily
Rub against my skin

Please baby, try to understand why
Please baby, look into my eyes

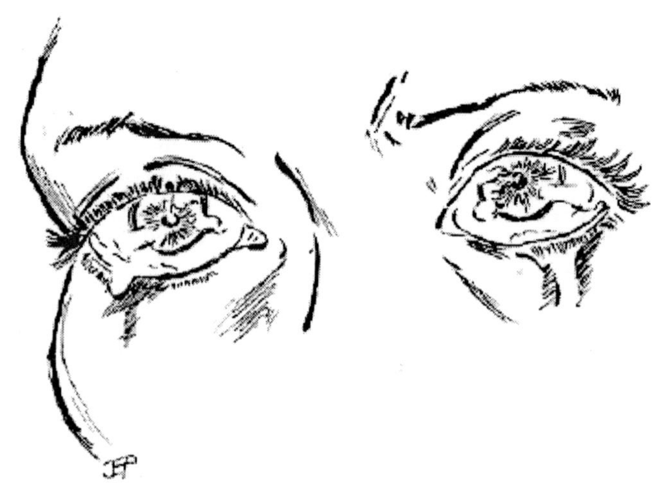

Shelbie M. Moore

Why Is It Bad When I Do It?

When they do it
It's fine
It's cool
It's erotic even

Two heads of hair
Two precious smiles
Two mesmerizing eyes
Two girls

They laugh
They hold hands
They kiss
Men smile

But when I do it
It's wrong
It's disgusting
It's disgraceful even

Two pairs of muscles
Two gangsta bodies
Two masculine smiles
Two guys

We laugh
We hold hands
We kiss
They laugh

So…
You may see why
I wish to keep
This a secret

Because we deserve
Better
So much better
Than what they give us

Shelbie M. Moore

Being The Other Girl

As you lay with me
And I kiss on you, so gentle
You say you love me
And I believe it's truthful

Then you button up your pants
Walk out the door
And I'm left feeling like
A common little whore

I called your house
To hear you say hello
But your woman was home
So you had to go

My friends tell me to leave you
My mama says I'm stupid
My daddy wants to kill you
Ugh! I fucking hate cupid!

With his bows and his arrows
With his matches in his head
He puts people in love
By the list he swears he read

But he must have messed up
Because he made a man love two
Well, he claims he loves me
And I swear it's true

Don't Turn Down The Radio

I'm sorry, can you turn the music up?
I don't like it quiet
I don't like the silence
It makes me think
It makes me remember

Compared to the average person
My life was simple
Good home, good school
But
Bad memories
Memories you don't know
Memories you couldn't imagine
Memories I can't tell you

And, when I remember
These memories
I cry
And when I cry
I can't sleep
And when I can't sleep
I lie awake
And I think
And I remember

So, I'm sorry,
Can you turn the music up?

Shelbie M. Moore

Left Turn At Me

As you walk away
I follow you
Chase you down
Plead for your forgiveness
Only to have you run away
Again
And again
I'll chase you

Well
My feet hurt
My legs are sore
So I'm gonna slow down
And maybe I'll stop
And maybe I'll turn around
And maybe
Just maybe
You'll look back
To see
If I'm still chasing after you

Shelbie M. Moore

Raped

I was raped
Not raped of my childhood
But of my happiness
And of the hope
That maybe he could love me
Maybe he would think back
And talk to me again

I was raped
Not by a drug abuser
By a born loser
Someone I thought
That would call me again
Or pick up a pen
And write to me
Saying he was sorry

I was raped
Not by a mad man
By a sad man
Who didn't like me
Who wanted me until he had me
Then he disappeared on me
He played me
Not even thinking
That with him
I was happy

I was raped
Not by a liar
By a story teller
Someone who wanted to be able to say
I had her once
And I could again

Oh how I wish
He could just pick up a pen
And tell me he was sorry
For raping me

Shelbie M. Moore

Homemade Dishes

…poems about being unique

Choosing to Snap

I didn't choose to be different
It's just how I am
I know how annoying I get
When I want chicken and not ham

It's really not my fault
Hip-hop pleases me more than rock
I apologize for the inconvenience
If I prefer flop-flops over socks

And excuse my rudeness
When all of you clap
That I lift my fingers
And choose to snap

Snap once for effort
Snap two for respect
Snap three or four for greatness
And five for being different

I see snapping as an old trait
Poets usually do
I'm just changing the snaps' meaning
Into to some original and new

But if I'm a little late
And someone has done it in the past
They had a good idea
And I'm making sure it last

                    Shelbie M. Moore

Pro-Me

He did use protection
But a hole was in the tip
I can't believe I didn't check
How could I have been so stupid!

Vomiting eight weeks later
Tired all the time
My baby had a heartbeat
The size of a dime

I was a junior in high school
28 was my ACT score
I knew who I was
But I was still called a whore

Yes I was pro-choice
Yes I was not ready
Yes my parents were mad
Yes my relationship was unsteady

Ten months passed by
And my body had healed
As I took home schooled classes
My baby still squealed

But ten years later
My son was in school
And just like his daddy
He loved to act a fool

I was happy when he was a senior
When he scored a 24
When he was accepted to college
When he walked out my door

I'm still not pro-life
Because I wanted a choice
I chose to be a mother
And give my child a voice

                              Shelbie M. Moore

I'll Prove You Wrong

Are ya'll whispering softly
About my man and me
Say it to my face
All the things you're hiding from me

You think he's a liar
A cheater and a bad guy
And you said he's screwing me over
Did you see it with your own eyes?

Do you know what he's said?
What he's doing or what he did?
What about the to concern he's shown for me
Or the bets he hasn't bid?

I'm sorry, did you say no?
Of course you said it
Don't open up your mouth
Because I'm not finished yet

I finally have a good guy
To stand by my side
If I'm driving away
He's down for the ride

I trust him to have friends
Who happen to be women
Because he can trust me enough
To have friends who are men

I'm sorry y'all got players
And pimps and thugs
I apologize that my lame man
Is into books and not drugs

So step child, step!
Because I sick of the mess
And the problems you're starting
With the couple who's the best

Now I am finished
Conversing with you
I got places to be
And better things to do

Shelbie M. Moore

Beautiful Disaster

How can something be beautiful
And be called a disaster
It's something very confusing
But easy to master

A person seems blissful
All loving and fine
But you need to look deeper
Inside their soul and mind

They are hurting so badly
They are in shock
In disbelief, in awe
They feel like a ticking clock

They want their life to end
So they can't weep anymore
They want to see if heaven
Can really heal their sores

They are like a song
With a hidden message
Like a older woman
Hiding her age

They don't want to be noticed
Yet they want to scream
So they feel it's easier
To be beautiful and unseen

You're A Bitch!

Yes, I am a bitch
I'm a
beautiful, irreplaceable, talented, compassionate and honest
Lady

And yes, sometimes I can be a
Bitter, immature, testy, classless and hurtful
Little girl

But I'm a rich bitch
I'm rich in creativity, worship and life
In feelings, humor and intellect
In fashion, bravery, and sympathy

But you
You are so sad
Because you had to stoop so low
As to take society's word
For a female dog
And say it to my face
And mean it to be painful

But, you see
I'm taking our word back
As a compliment

And you
My fellow bitch
Have made me see
That us rich bitches
Can fill a poor woman's body
With a great amount of jealousy

So now
You have just turned me
Into a
bigger, interesting, tongue twisting, conceited and heart
warming
B-I-T-C-H

                                    Shelbie M. Moore

Confidence

The power to say
I am me
No matter what you see

Power is a privilege
To be you
To trust yourself
To help yourself

Belief
In one's self
Finding someone
To show confidence
In you

Confidence
An impulse
So fragile
That it must be handled
With the most care

I want to give you
The confidence
To have the power
To say
You are you
And I am me

Confidence
Is what you should see
In our children
Who will have
The power
To change history

Shelbie M. Moore

What My Body Would Say

Love my soul
Make me happy
Accept my mind
Respect the inner me

I am a temple
To be worshiped and adored
Not something you can come to
Whenever you get bored

No disrespect
To the man of hip-hop
But this girl doesn't like
The taste of the lollipop

Call me back boy
If I call you first
Not in the dark morning
To look up my skirt

I'm not about to let you
Hit it and quit it
I'm too good for that
And I'm ready to admit it

Thanks Again

My relations with you
Did last very long
I still think about you
When I hear a love song

But I guess I'm grateful
You helped me out a lot
You gave most of my poems
A really good plot

You helped me realize
You're a great advisor
And since I am alone
I know I am wiser

Now I am stronger, energetic
And so much happier too
This happened because of our past
So, again, I thank you

Shelbie M. Moore

I wonder

I sat on my porch
Just watching the night sky
Only watching

I looked at the stars
Just starring into the blackness
Only starring

I rocked in my chair
Just thinking about life
Only thinking

I hummed a tune I heard
Just wondering what's out there
Only wondering

"I wonder if he sees the same moon?"
Just asking myself that repetitive question
Only asking

Wondering the answer
Hopefully awaiting in the stars

Lip Singing Fool

And as the school day progresses
I hear a new name every hour
However, once I go home
I go to my room with the shower

It's my little oasis
With a radio and a mirror
Where I can be a diva
A pop star and a singer

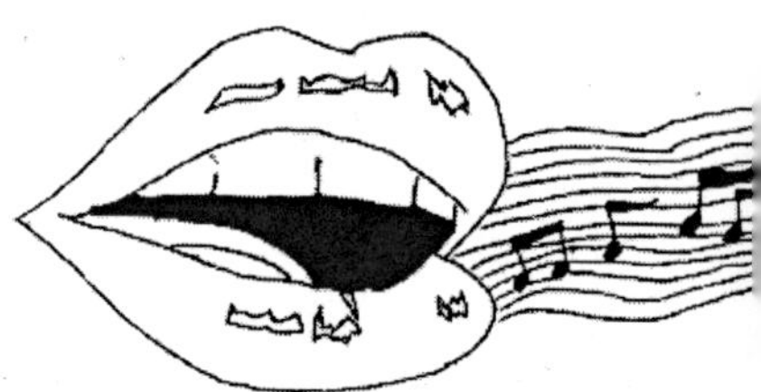

I blast my stereo high
I grab my comb or brush
I lift it to my lips
And sing about my crush

T.I or Saving Abel
Sweet Dreams or *So What?*
I just kick and scream
Like a crazy little nut

And once my dream is over
I fix up my hair
And I smile at my satisfaction
Which has become so rare

Because I have defeated the hype
I had rebelled against the cool
I can be what I want to be
Which is a lip singing fool

Shelbie M. Moore

Am I Weird?

Am I weird
Because when a teacher tells me to be quiet I listen?
Am I weird
Because when my mother tells me something I pay attention?

Am I weird
Because I don't use degrading terms on my friends?
Am I weird
If I return something I borrowed even if it was only a pen?

Am I weird
Because I make my homework easy to ready for my
professors?
Am I weird
Because I treat my family as if they were all powerful and
royal ancestors?

Am I weird?
Am I abnormal?
Am I lame?
No. I'm respectable

A Chair

When we sit down
We sit in a chair

Just a chair

The legacy of the chair
Is one to be foretold by every generation

It started as a seat
Then we put the seat on wheels
Then we put those wheels on a bike
That bike became a car
That car became a plane
That plane became a spaceship
That spaceship took us to the moon

Queens and kings have one
Killers have one
Children have one
Different ones, of course
But a chair none the less

So
The next time you look at something
Don't think, it's just *this* or it's just *that*

Because a chair
Is more than *just* a chair
Like everything this world
It belongs somewhere

Shelbie M. Moore

Hoodie and Nikes

It was raining the last time I looked outside
So I grabbed my hoodie
The grass and sidewalks were flooding over
So I grabbed my old Nikes

In the past, being trapped in a room didn't bother me
So I stayed in my bed
As the days turned into weeks, I got really bored
So I poured the thoughts out of my head

Being sick and tired makes you sick and tired
And I'm tired of being sick
I'm not terminally ill or dying
But that's what I'd rather pick

As a person who is carefree and calm
I don't care a lot about what people say
But when you're trapped in a crowed room
It's very hard to look away

"You better do this, you better do that"
"I don't see how you don't get it"
My head hurts, my eyes are dry
I'm getting tired of this shit!

Always crying! Always screaming!
But smiling in their presence
Time passes and the wounds heal
And all seems well with a kiss

But I still feel trapped inside
I'm still sick, tired, and in shame
So I'm gonna grab my hoodie and Nikes
And go running in the rain

Chocolate Covered Cherries

Sweet Nothings

...those lovely dovey poems we all adore

                    Shelbie M. Moore

Dear Darling

How is it,
The curl of your lips,
And the rock of your hips,
Are so hard to resist?

How can I,
Not stare at you in class,
And not look as you pass,
With my wandering eye?

How can we,
Not say a word all day,
But I laugh at what you say,
Oh, how can I make you see?

That, my baby,
You are the love of my life,
The joy of my strife,
And the yes when I say maybe

Chocolate

Busy Bodies

We both have a schedule
To memorize and maintain
We both have jobs to do
Whether it hails or it rains

There are bills to pay
And kids to raise
Groceries to buy
And lords to praise

We have to call our clients
Take all of our pills
Even some extra vitamins
Because we can't afford to get ill

But, when we said *I do*
We made a solid vow
To stay together forever
Starting with right now

So once we're all done
Doing what we need to do
Let's schedule some time
For just me and you

Shelbie M. Moore

The Little Things

You know me well
Which is why you are mine
You know I love cupcakes
And the smell of pine

You know about my ticklish spot
Rich under my belly button
You know my worst blemish
Is the birthmark under my chin

You've memorized all my CDs
From my greatest adored to my least
You know for Thanksgiving
I don't like those big feasts

And you know when I'm mad
You can always make me beam
By kissing my left cheek
And calling my your sweet thing

How you figured all this out
I never want to understand
I'm just happy you did
And I love that you're my man

Lovely Little Emotion
(From my novel "Just a Little Boy Crazy")

My emotion took me over
Rushing inside and out
Like lightning
Crash! Bang! Ahh!
Pushing me back and forth
Up and down
We both went
Cotton and nylon
Under our bodies
And piled on the floor
Tangled in a twist
Like our arms and our kiss
The door was locked
My mother's face told me
Stop! Don't do it honey!
He ain't worth it!
And I thought
If this man can control me
Like this lovely little emotion taking over me
I don't ever want him to leave me
I just want him to squeeze me
And give me his time
I want him to become mine
I want this
Lovely little emotion
To be with him
Like it is with me
I wanted to be the first to say to him
I'm not gonna leave you
Like they did baby
I'm gonna stay
Because you give me
This lovely little emotion
That I don't ever want to go away

                    Shelbie M. Moore

Tessa

Nicholas Sparks called his masterpiece
"The Notebook"
He said it was neither a romance
Or a tragedy
But that is was a little of both
That was Tessa

Her life was the mess
That mothers and fathers
Warn their daughters about

When I think of Tessa
I think of a strong woman
But a scared girl
Who had a baby

A baby is the best blessing
A woman and a man can receive
And conceive
But when you lose that baby
Your world comes crashing down

The tragedy is
The baby was gone
She doesn't remember
Because she doesn't want to

The romance is
He stuck around
To care for her
And raise their second child
With as much love as the first

He stood by her
Through everything
Like a man
Like her man
Like Noah did for Allie

Shelbie M. Moore

Unfaithful

Before I become addicted to your
Deception
Before I become absorbed with your
Inspiration
Before my mistakes
Become our perfection
I want to become tired of you

Your scent
Your strength
Your hands
So soft they could
Comfort a crying child
Who's lost it's mother
I am the child
To your womb
Let me get tired of you soon

I remember the first time we made love
Before we had sex
How my emotions transferred
From bad, to good, to the next . . .
I need to get tired of you

The only way to end this
Is for one of us
To get tired

And as much as I
Hope and pray
It will have to be
You

Because
My sweet addiction
I'll never get tired of you

Let Me Make It Up To You

My time is done baby
I'm done acting crazy
I'm a man of our lord
Let me back in your door

Come and reminisce
About our hug and our kiss
Our special night and song
Forget about the things done wrong

Baby, I've changed
Baby, I ain't the same
I'm different from the past
I'm better than the last

Let's go back in time
When I was yours and you were mine
Baby, come and take a walk with me
Come and set my body free

The Puppy and The Kitten

A lovely golden kitten
She drank the whitest of milk
She ate the finest food
She wore the smoothest silk

A dirty brown puppy
Ate his food out the trash
He drank from the sewers
He gave everyone a rash

The kitten was bored of her life
She decided she wanted fun
The puppy was scared of the night
So he ran toward the sun

Some how these babies met
At a fountain in the park
Together they sang songs
She meowed and he barked

The two kids became happy
So they ran away together
They never went back home
And they fell in love with each other

Shelbie M. Moore

Upendi

Upendi is energy
A passionate energy

Imagine a wind
A strong wind
A wind that wraps around you
So very gentle

It cuddles you
Well, more like caresses you
Starting at your toes
Working your way up your legs
That ribbon of wind
Ties around your heart

When Upendi reaches your heart
You're helpless
You surrender your body to it
You fall
And you hope someone catches you

If someone catches you
Upendi has captured you too

The World I See

When I turn around
I see you
You
Are so beautiful
Hair eyes skin nose
My God
You are perfect

But I look forward
The world
Baby girl, it's a scary place

The hatas coming my way
Tryin to spit game your way
Disin on the things I say
Tryin to keep you away
They wanna call you baby
I'm not having that

Every corner I turn
I view the world
They tease us
Try to please us
Bending down on their knees
Just to hit the shins
Of the things
Holding us up
I don't want that

Shelbie M. Moore

Every breathe I take
I take in their taste and smell
The odors and bitterness of hell
The things they stole and trying to sell
To me
To be like them
I don't need that

Then you take my hand
And when I turn around
I see you
You
Are so beautiful
Hair eyes skin nose
My God
You are perfect

You are my world
The only world I need to see

Two bodies, One Beat

Stepping together
Moving as one
Clothes spinning
Fingers over thumbs

Heels clacking
Smiles forming
Switching positions
Bodies soaring

Hair twisting
Music changing
Eyes starring
Moods rearranging

Arms around the neck
Hands on the hips
Thanks for the dance
Now how about a kiss?

The North Star

My parents once told me
"If you ever lose your phone
Follow the North Star
To take you back home"

"Not only can it do that
But it has magic powers
Far beyond the galaxy
And past the meteor showers"

"But mama," I asked.
"What do you mean?
How can a star led me home
When all it does is gleam?"

"I wanted proof too baby
When my mama said the same thing
One night I heard the star whisper
Follow me past the stream"

"And my mama was right child
Because once I followed that star farther
I meet a man who'd lost his keys
And now you call him father"

                          Shelbie M. Moore

**Define Love
(From Me to You)**

Love is just a word
Love has no description
Unless you find someone
To give it a definition

Before I met you
I was a dictionary missing a page
Before I met you
I was a poet going insane

Before I met you
My pencil wrote for a surplus
Now that I know you
My eraser has no purpose

You challenge me
You make me
Work my hardest
So I can be
The best first lady
That you ever called baby

Before I met you
Love was just four little letters
But now that I love you
Those letters are all that matter

What I'm Thinking

I know it sounds corny
Quite generic even
But I truly must express
The real way I'm feeling

You control my mind when I dream
You control it when I wake up
You make me feel gorgeous
With or without make up

I choose all my outfits
To fit your favorite colors
I get all your little secrets
From your lovely mother

I'd call you early if I could
So I'd be the first thing you hear
And, I'd love it too if
You whispered "Good Morning" in my ear

Love is not an option
Because it's way to soon
But if I had to choose you or our galaxy
I wouldn't miss that full moon

                    Shelbie M. Moore

My Good Senses

I lick my lips
Hoping your taste will still be there
I rub my head
Hoping to feel your hands in my hair

I smell the air
Sniffing for your cologne
I think of the time
When we were all alone

I chuckle and I smile
And think about our parents
Who, when they found out,
Told us we'd loss our senses

I remember mocking them and saying
"All my senses are fine
I know all of his now
And he knows all of mine"

Chocolate Covered Cherries

Did you ever want to try a dessert?
A sweet, sugary dessert
Like a cherry
Dipped in chocolate
And you just wanted a taste
A tiny taste
Just to say you tasted it
Finally tasted it

I've wanted that chocolate covered cherry
I've wanted it for a long time
That tempting fruit
Dipped in my favorite topping
I've dreamt of it
For so many years

I finally had the chance
My last chance
To let that sweet treat
Roll around in my mouth
I would been satisfied
So satisfied
With just a tiny taste
But my stomach growled with anger
And pulled me back

I wanted to say to my stomach,
"Is it so wrong
To want to try
A chocolate covered cherry
That you've always wanted to taste
Even before you even had
That great piece of humble pie
Waiting for you at home?"

                    Shelbie M. Moore

Metaphorically Speaking

Stepping on knifes
Pulling down the drape
To cover this hour glass shape
Living everyone elses' lives

This is why I'm glad to have you
To make me feel healthy and rested

You're my doctor
You're my therapist
You're my husband
You're my everything

In Love With Love

I love You
Wow that feels good
Man, I mean that feels really good
That feels great!

Is this what it feels like?
All these emotions at once?

This happiness when you smile
And I'm the one to cause it!
This sensation I get
When you wrap your arms around my waist!

Baby! Say it!
You love me too?
That's so nice of you
I never heard anyone say that to me before
That must be what it feels like to be insecure
I don't like that feeling

You're gonna take it away?
Thank you baby!
You don't know what you do to me
You make me so happy!

This must be what my mama and daddy have
What my Grandfolks got
What Family Matters and Jada and Will keep
Good God!
I love love!
I'm in love with love!
And man, it feels good

                                    Shelbie M. Moore

Full Courses

...poems about laughter, lessons and life

Why Did I Say No?

When I was miserable
He was there for me
When I had no one
He was my everybody

However, he was different
He was outgoing
He invited to me to parties
And I was afraid of showing

When he finally asked me
To be his one and only
My heart wanted to say yes
But my brain said to stay lonely

My brain said to say no
Because it knew better
My heart said to say yes
But it didn't want to shatter

My thinking and love muscles
Might not ever agree
But somehow they'll always know
What my answer should be

Shelbie M. Moore

Future Promise

Our teacher assigned a project
And I really needed an A
"Write a poem about the future," he said.
"And nothing too cliché"

It was due the next morning
And I was totally unprepared
I didn't know what to write
So at my paper, I just stared

My mother walked in
Explaining the details of her date
She did this every night
No matter how late

As she left with a smile
I wondered about my dad
All the memories we shared
And the ones we could have had

After the divorce I wondered,
"Why didn't they stay together?"
Then I finally knew
What I'd put in my letter

With this ring, I wrote
I do thee wed
That is what
I promised and said

So with this ring
I swear once more
To stay together
No matter what's in store

Chocolate Covered Cherries

In sickness and health
'Till death do us part
I promise to keep you
Engraved in my heart

So in the future
Maybe these terms
Will still be in the world
To be honored and learned

Shelbie M. Moore

A New Title

There are poets
There are songwriters
There are rappers
There are play-writers

They most definitely have
A great gift with a pen
And they are all very
Emotional humans

Every single one
Makes their checks
By thinking extra hard
And creating new couplets

A teenage mother once wrote
"I know why the cadged bird sings"
The first black man on MTV sung
"P.Y.T; pretty young thing"

Different stories
Different ways
Different clothes
Different names

Their lyrics are spun
Into a certain style
With various themes
That can be important or vile

They're all unique
They're all vital
They just have jobs
With different titles

Chocolate Covered Cherries

I don't understand why
Some people are so prejudice
They hate on things
They have no right to dis

Greatness is flowing
So open your mind up
Pick up a straw
And suck it up

Don't turn away
From the popular or new
Only because
It's not what you're used too

Please don't be so picky
Just to say you're different
If you really want to be original
Then pick up a pen

Shelbie M. Moore

I Need A Resolution

Dear Lord
Thank you
Thank you for everything you have done for me
For my friends
And for my family
And, as a new year begins
I will bow down before you
And give you my resolution
So you may process it again

Dear Lord
I'm tired
Every year it gets a little harder
And I'm tired
I need a way
To get some rest when I want
To eat when I want
To live when I want
So this year
My resolution is to be selfish

Dear Lord
Try to understand
I've helped raised my babies
Their babies
And *their* babies
Without my husband around, bless his soul
I'm fed up with trying to please everyone on my own
And I think I need time to relax
I want to have time to enjoy the wonderful world you created

Dear Lord
I need your help to carry out
My new year's resolution
Because my generosity won't let me do it alone
I need you to give me the courage
To say no
So I can live on
To say yes

Shelbie M. Moore

Done Asking

Comic books
Fantasies
Non fiction
And mysteries

Lines of words
Written on pages
Talking about life
In different stages

You don't have to write them
But you should open a book
Whether it's for entertainment
Or to learn how to cook

Reading is wack
Reading is gay
I'm tried of hearing excuses
That people tend to say

Are you acting white
Because you enjoy reading?
I'm telling you now
Because I'm done pleading

Pick up a book!
What's the big deal?
If you need someone to help you
Find someone who will!

Put some effort into
Your higher education!
And a few words to the parents . . .
Give your child some persuasion

                                    Shelbie M. Moore

Some Things Will Never Change

The equivalence of the human mind
Is oblivious to the human kind

Although our thoughts are never alike
Our actions hold the same spite

We all have revenge we want to seek
We all have goals we want meet

That pesky voice raping at our brains
Like that damn Raven driving that man insane

In the end it will wear us out
We must take the reins and learn to mount

Ride that thought to the very last beat
Ride that thought down the very last street

We all must come to reason
That once upon this time
Our minds will unwind
And then combine
To create
A world
That needs to
Precipitate
A rain coming down
On our narrow brains

It's the idea
That some things
Will remain the same

Those Men

Which is better
From your man
The calls and the text
The lovemaking, not sex
The squeezing of your hand
Or a love letter

Which is a better guy
One who cries with you
One who makes eye contact
One who knows how to act
One who is the father of two
Or one who doesn't lie

What about their job
Should they be rich
On welfare, illegal
Dirty hands, sterile
Paid to be a snitch
Or do they just rob

Picky little people
Want men perfect to the T
What ever happened to the romance
Not what's in the pants
Now it's all about the money
Not the steeple

A good man isn't hard to find
Just don't go after boys
Know when one likes you
When one really wants to be with you
Just wait to enjoy
The man of your kind

Shelbie M. Moore

Go Ahead and Smile

With a smile
I took on the world
With a smile
I felt like a little girl

I road my bike
From Cleveland to Tennessee
I took an old boat
Down the Mississippi

I took of my hat
And let my hair blow
I put on a coat
And played in the snow

I picked up some gloves
And planted many fruits
I grabbed a clean blender
And mixed the sweetest juice

I sat on my porch
And sipped my drink
And with a smile on my face
I closed my eyes to think

Fish Eye

Taken from my home
Placed into a shop
But, unlike my mother
I stayed out of the pot

A little girl took me away
From the other animals
Her mother let her keep me
Because I wasn't a mammal

They named me rose
But I was born may-sing
And through the water's waves
I could see everything

Her clothes, her hair
The phone calls she had
I remembered her face
When she'd done something bad

One time, she slammed her door
She wasn't allowed to leave
Her teacher swore she cheated
So she cried and grieved

I remember her studying
Until the break of day
I remember her praying
Begging God for an A

So, if I could testify
To prove her innocence
I'd jump off her dresser
Within two seconds

                                    Shelbie M. Moore

But as may-sing or rose
I am trapped in this place
Where no one will see
The truth on my face

Free Falling

Most times when I fall
I fall hard
And I prayed to god
That one day
He would
Give me someone
Would pick me up

But you?
You let me fall
Time and time again
You let me cry
So much that I almost forgot
What it felt like
To smile

You let me go home and think
"What did I do?
What have I done,
To deserve this torture?
This detention of sorrow?
This aggression that I must carry on tomorrow?"
Then I answered those rhetorical questions
With some common sense
"I did nothing."

Nothing as in
No work
No effort
No patience
No tolerance
No maturity
Nothing

So by asking God
For someone to pick me up
He gave me someone
To let me fall
So I learn to stand up on my own

He sent me someone
To grade my work with stars and zeros
He sent me
Someone who has taught me everyday
What it means to talk the right away
He sent me
Someone who calls my house
To tell my mother to be just proud of me
And don't judge me
But what she sees
Only when she looks at me

God sent me
A teacher
My teacher
Who I can never thank enough
For letting me fall

Shelbie M. Moore

Smile for the Camera

As I flip through the pictures
Of last month's magazines
I notice the painted nails
And the designer seams

Their eyebrows are arched
Their skin is perfectly shaded
But their smiles are the things
That keeps me turning pages

The models seem effortless
With those lips and teeth
They look almost flawless
But take a look underneath

500 frames
5,000 flashes
The frustration from hair
To fake eyelashes

They're human too
Their bodies are probably tired
They might just want to go home
And take a long and hot shower

And how do we thank them?
By bending their pages
By tearing them, folding them
And messing up those perfect faces

As I see the front covers
My mind gets all choppy
I think we've become so ungrateful that
We only reward the final copy

Chocolate Covered Cherries121

Heart Rate

When the ball dribbles
And its passed to me
My heart jumps up
And skips its beat

When I spin on the floor
In front of the crowd
My blood pumps higher
Than it should be allowed

While I help the patients
Into the ambulance
My veins start to pulse
Out of my goose-bumped skin

As I scream playfully
At my stage partner
A bump beats against my chest
Harder and harder!

The paint splashes around
And moves between my fingers
It would make my monitor
Shake, rattle and trigger

Some things you do
Just to pay bills
Other people do things
At their free will

No matter what the thing is
Such as sports or art
Find the one thing in your life
To make your heart rate star

                                        Shelbie M. Moore

Life

The ones we love
Are the ones we lose
Because we can not lose
The ones who do not like
For they are already lost

Yes, the ones we don't like
We might never love
But the ones we love
We might never like

Like a father and a mother
Perfect?
Never
Respect them?
Have too

Because
No matter what they did wrong
They did something right
They gave us life
They gave us pain
They gave us struggle
They made us grow

And for that
We can not hate them
We have to respect them
For they took the time
To let us like
And let us lose
The ones we loved

We stilled loved some
Before they were lost
And we have to respect
Something we will lose in the future
A gift
Which is something given to us
By people we may not like
The gift is
Life

                    Shelbie M. Moore

About the Author

Shelbie M Moore was born in Detroit, Michigan in 1992. This is the third book she has written. Shelbie enjoys cooking and loves eating. That is where she found the inspiration for the theme of this collection of poetry. Her favorite dessert is *almost* anything dipped in chocolate; including cherries. Shelbie wants to go to college to study Education, English, and/or Creative Writing.

Other Books by Shelbie M. Moore

Words Scribbled In My Notebook (2008)
-Poetry

Just A Little Boy Crazy (2009)
-Young Adult Novel

Keep In Contact With Shelbie M. Moore!

Scroll Through Her Blog,
The Fairy's Quill
At
www.ShelbieMMoore.wordpress.com
A Home for
Poets & Authors

Email Shelbie Anytime At:
ShelbieMMoore@gmail.com

LaVergne, TN USA
11 December 2009
166733LV00001B/9/P